A whitewashed pepperpot lighthouse marks where the Caledonian Canal joins Loch Lochy near Gairlochy

THE GREAT GLEN WAY

The Great Glen Way is one of Scotland's Great Trails and follows the course of the Caledonian Canal through the Highlands from Fort William to Inverness over up to 79 miles (124km). The waymarked trail includes easy, level stretches, undulating forest tracks, lakeside paths and old drove and military roads as well as high-level alternatives for those looking for a greater challenge. Typically taking a week, it is an ideal introduction to long-distance walking.

Contents and using this guide

This booklet of Ordnance Survey 1:25,000 Explorer® maps has been designed for convenient use on the trail and includes:

- a key to map pages (pages 2–3) showing where to find the maps for each stage.
- the full and up-to-date line of the trail.
- an extract from the OS Explorer map legend (pages 42–44).

The companion guidebook – *The Great Glen Way* – describes the full route in both directions with lots of other practical and historical information.

Cicerone's EU representative for GPSR compliance is Easy Access System Europe, Mustamäe tee 50, 10621 Tallinn, Estonia. Email gpsr.requests@easproject.com.

© Cicerone Press 2025
Second edition 2025
ISBN: 978 1 78631 142 9
First edition 2016
© Crown copyright and database rights 2025 OS AC0000810376
Photos © Paddy Dillon 2016
Printed in China on responsibly sourced paper on behalf of Latitude Press Ltd.

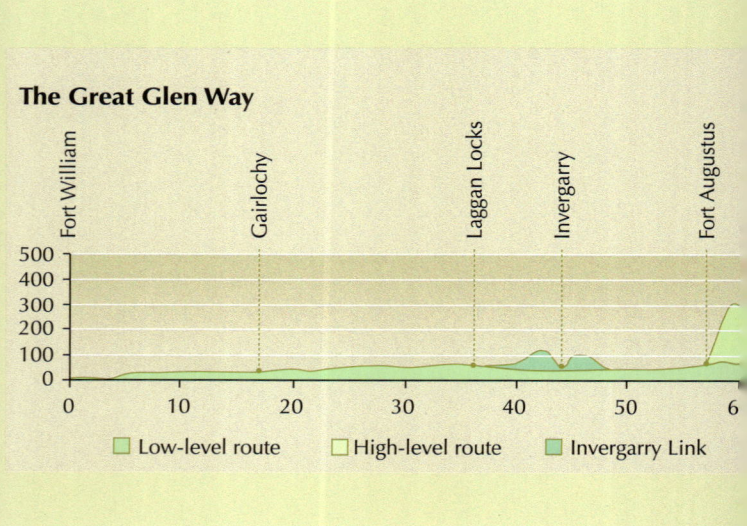

THE GREAT GLEN WAY

Stage 1	Fort William to Gairlochy	6
Stage 2	Gairlochy to Laggan Locks	10
Stage 3	Laggan Locks to Fort Augustus	17

Invergarry Link

Stage 2A	Gairlochy to Invergarry	16
Stage 3A	Invergarry to Fort Augustus	18
Stage 4A	Fort Augustus to Invermoriston (high-level)	22
Stage 4B	Fort Augustus to Invermoriston (low-level)	22
Stage 5A	Invermoriston to Drumnadrochit (high-level)	26
Stage 5B	Invermoriston to Drumnadrochit (low-level)	26
Stage 6	Drumnadrochit to Inverness	32

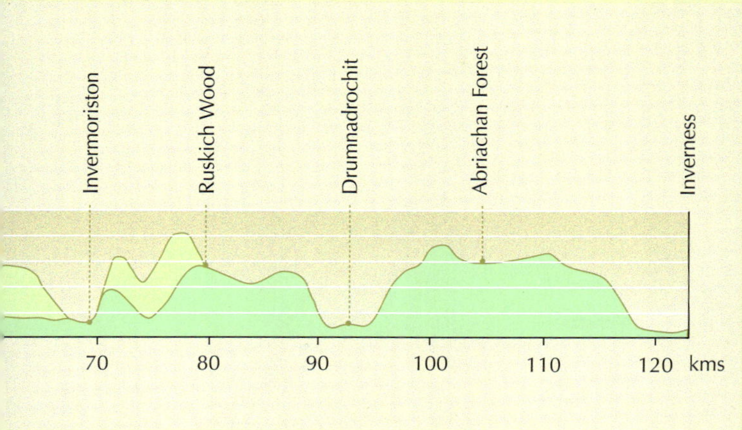

5

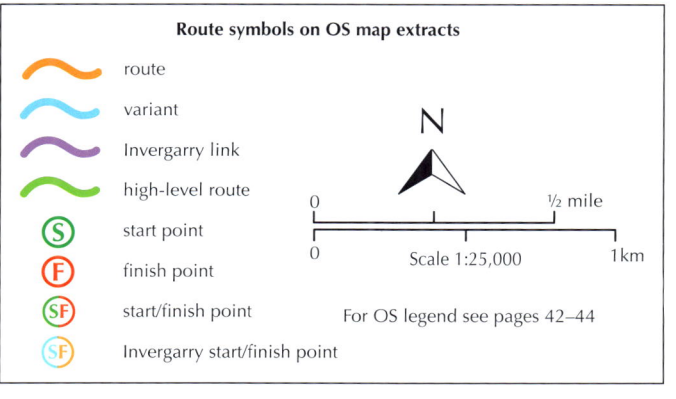

Route symbols on OS map extracts

- ～ route
- ～ variant
- ～ Invergarry link
- ～ high-level route
- Ⓢ start point
- Ⓕ finish point
- ⓈⒻ start/finish point
- ⓈⒻ Invergarry start/finish point

N

Scale 1:25,000
0 — ½ mile
0 — 1km

For OS legend see pages 42–44

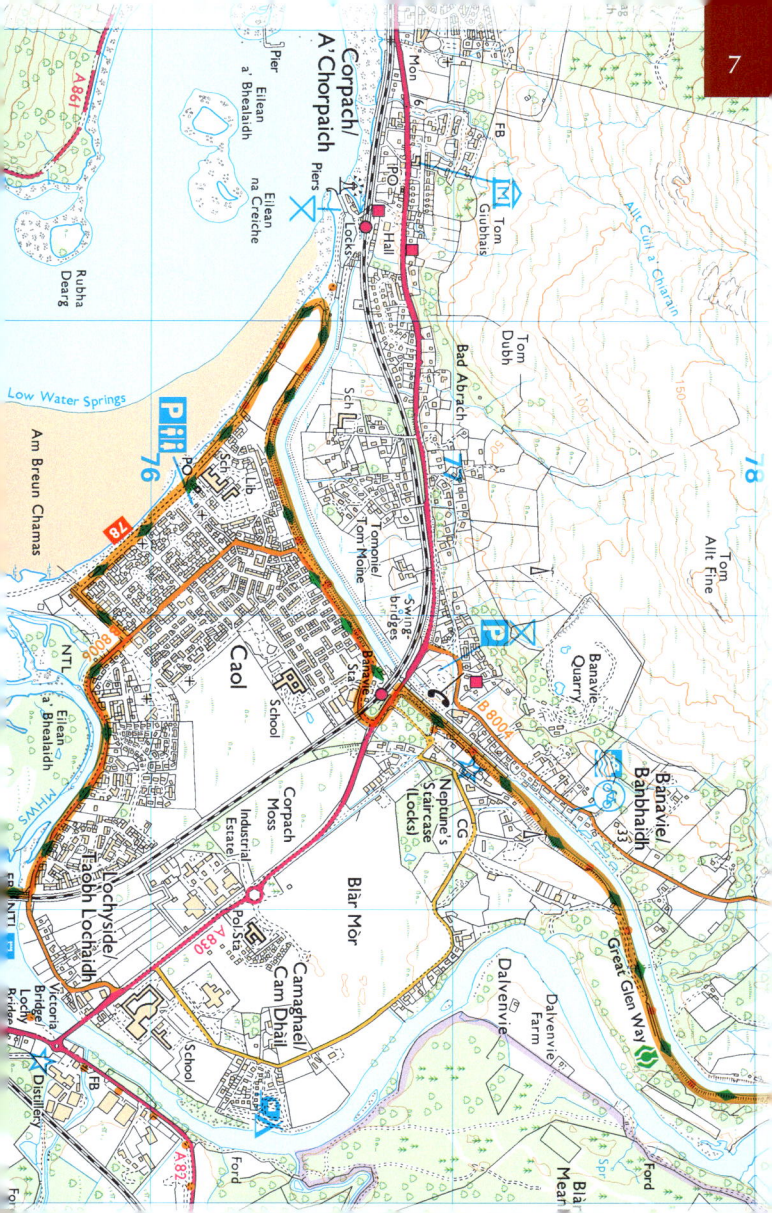

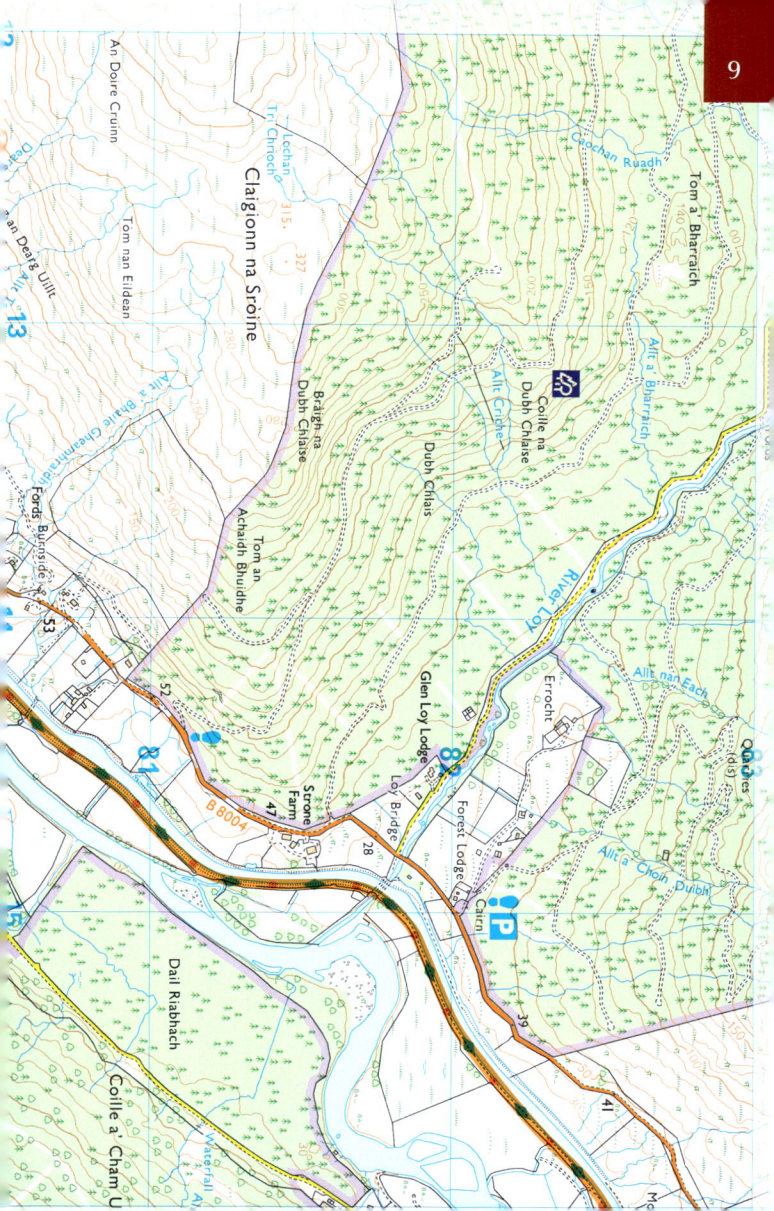

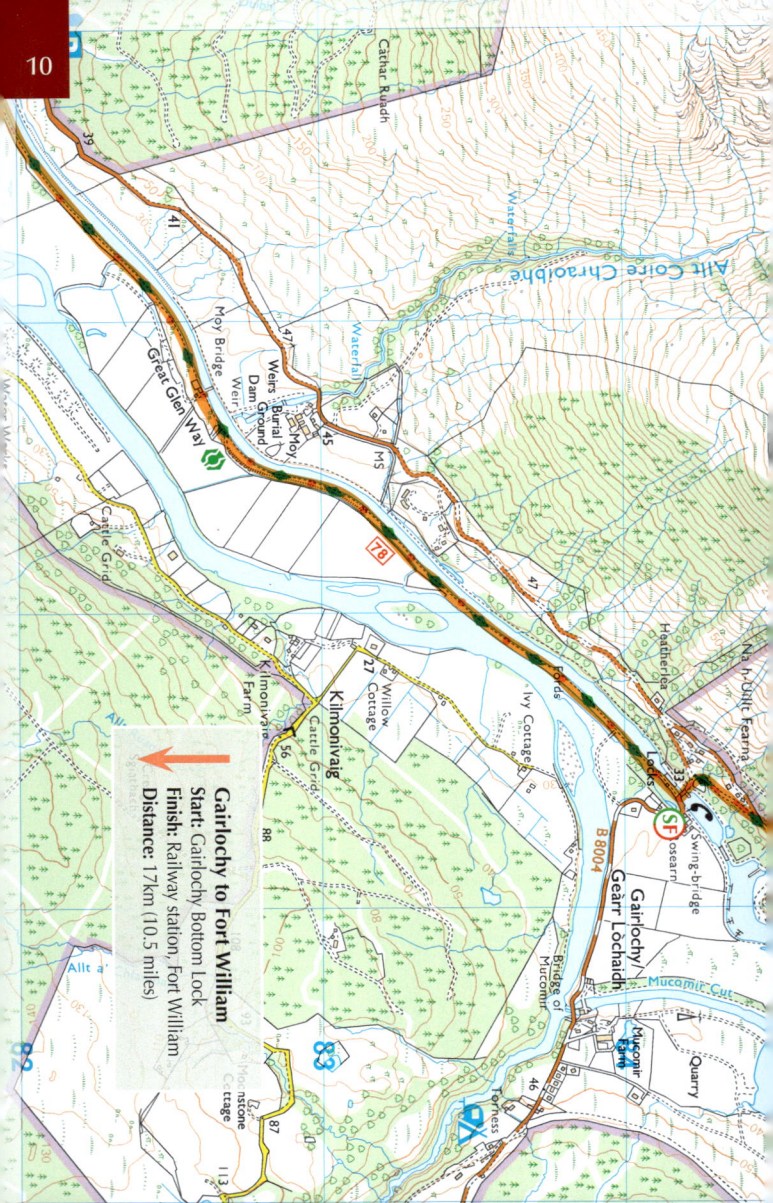

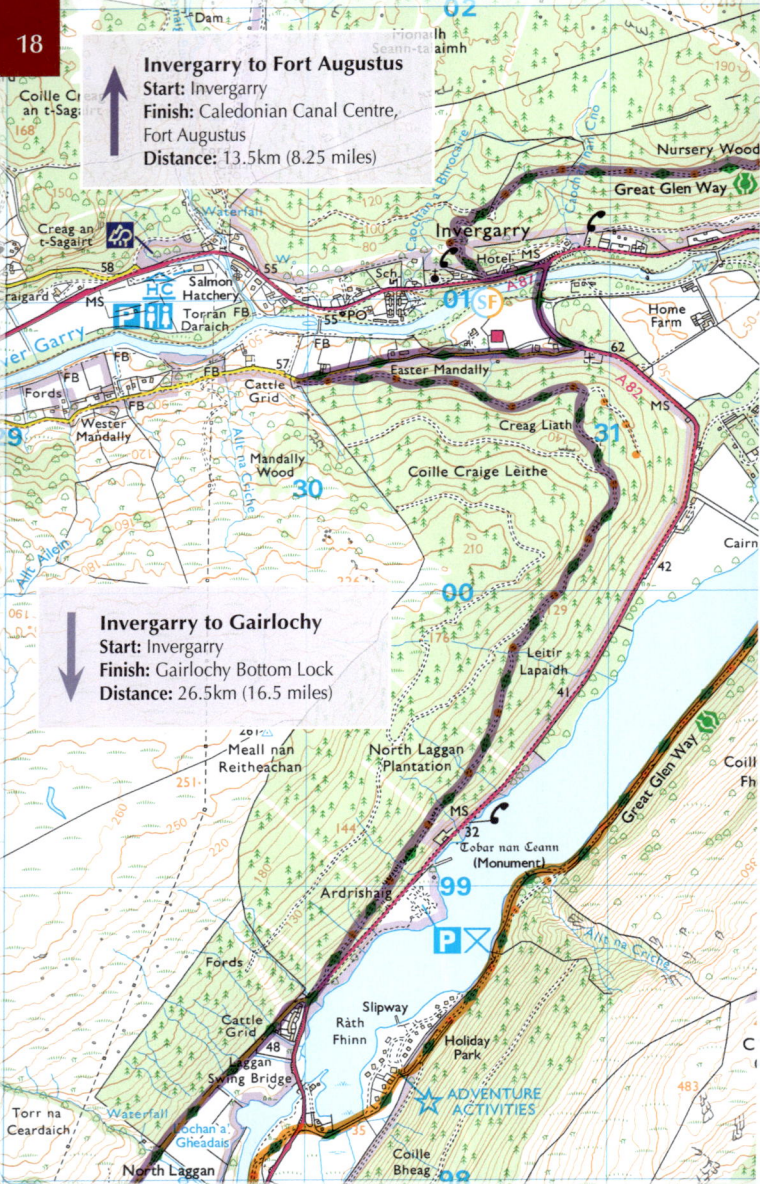

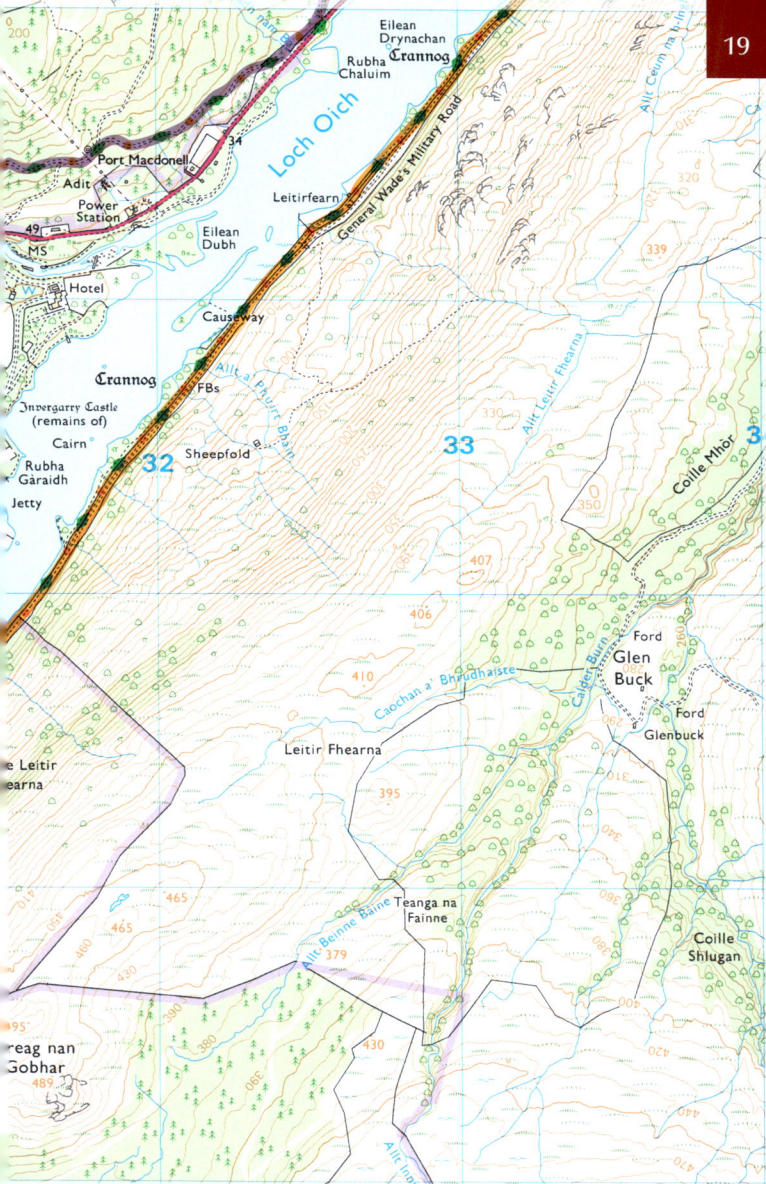

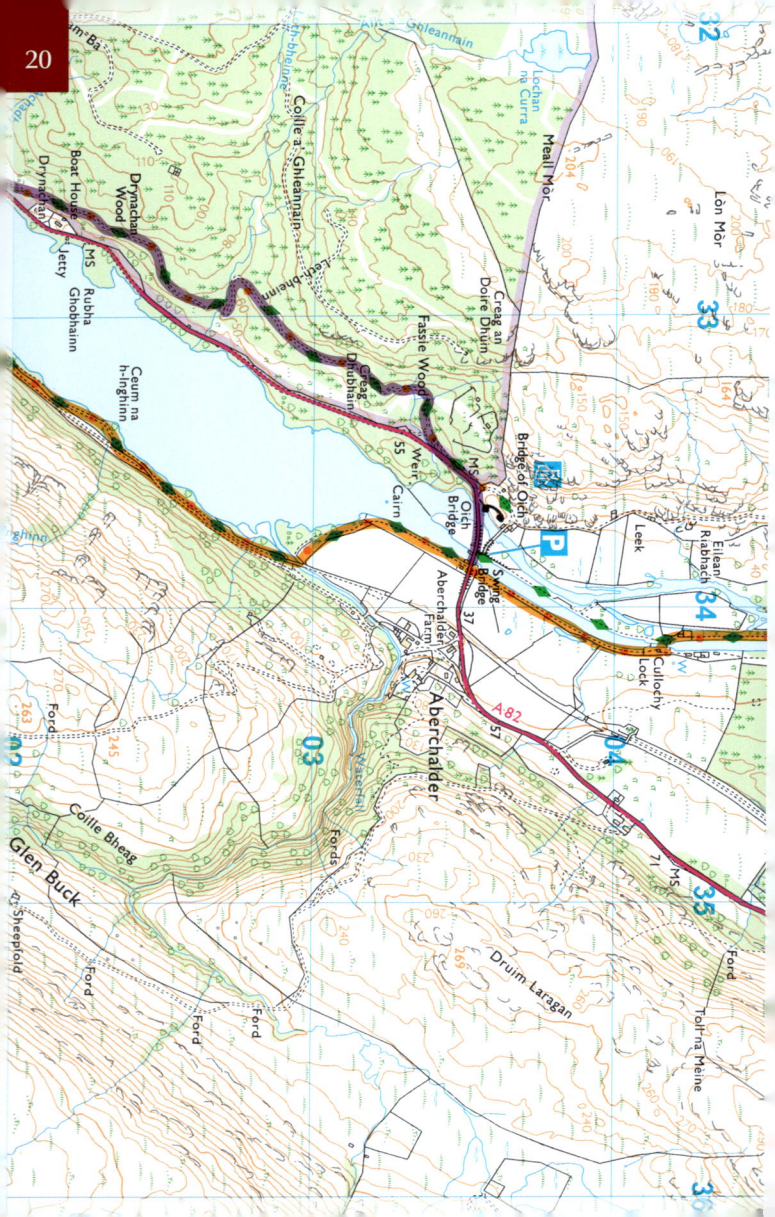

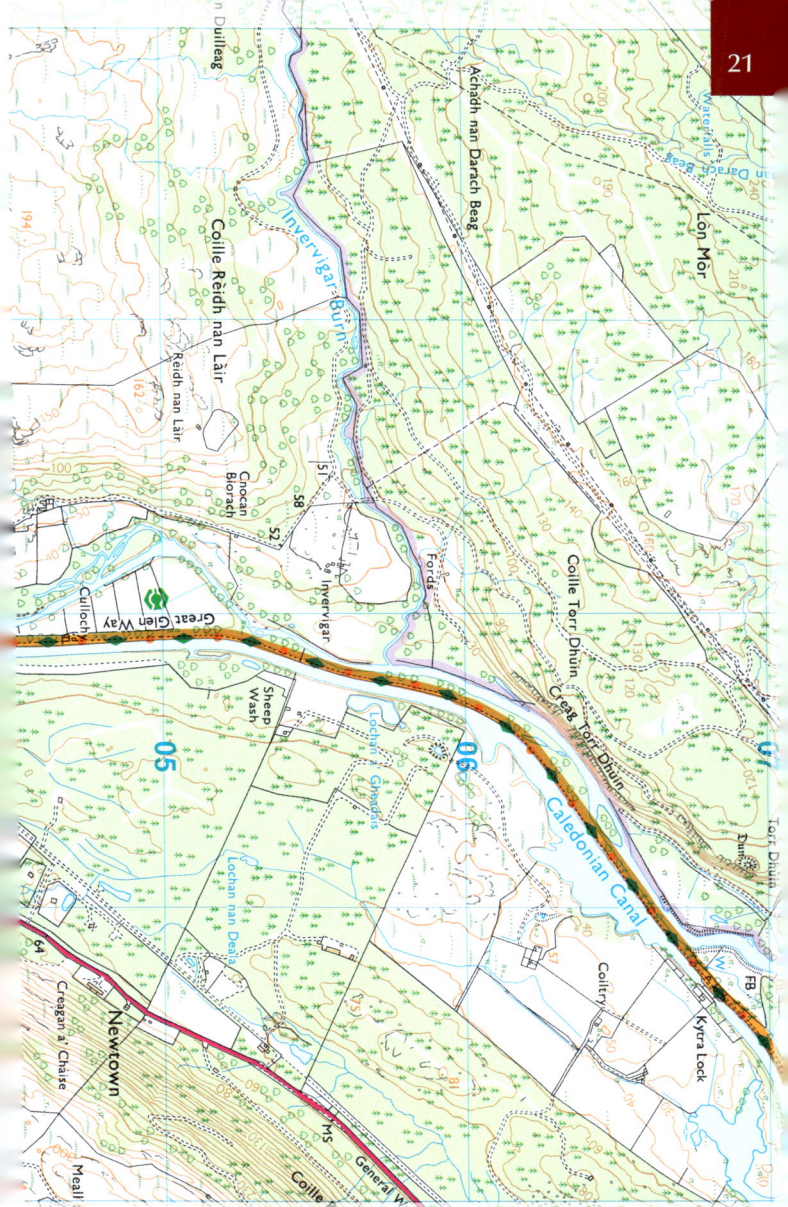

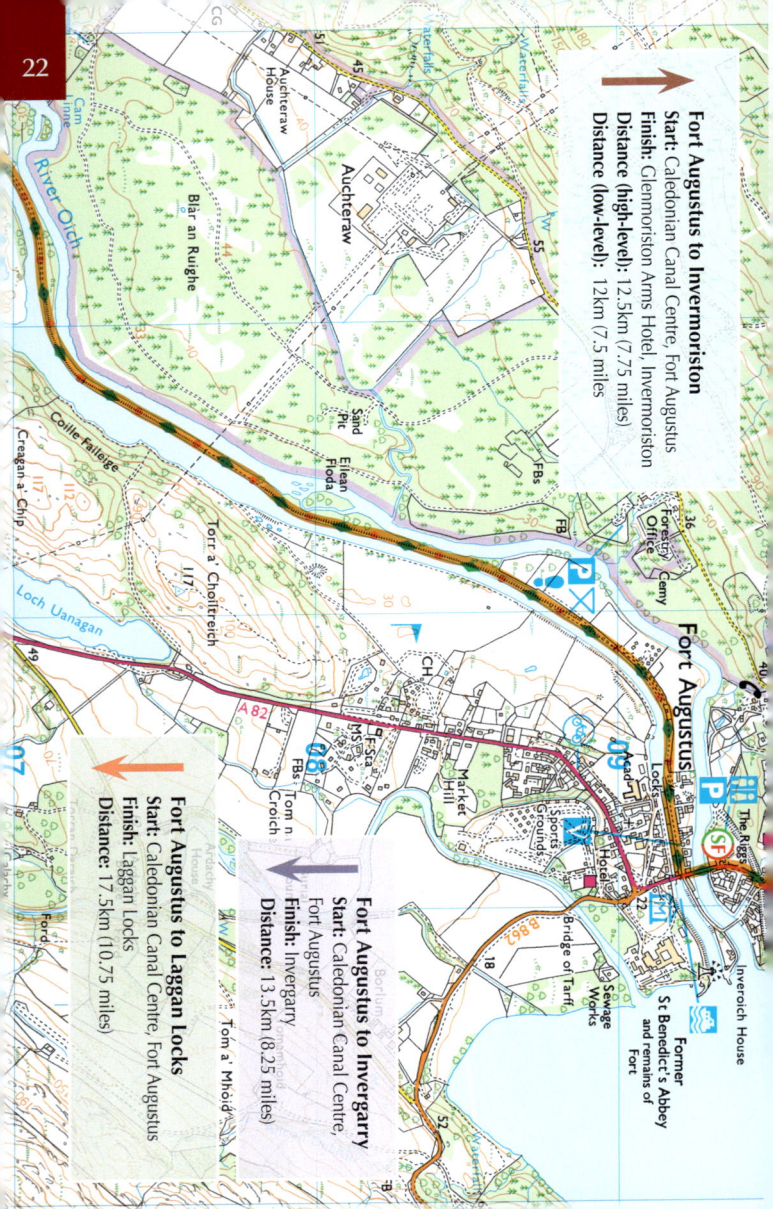

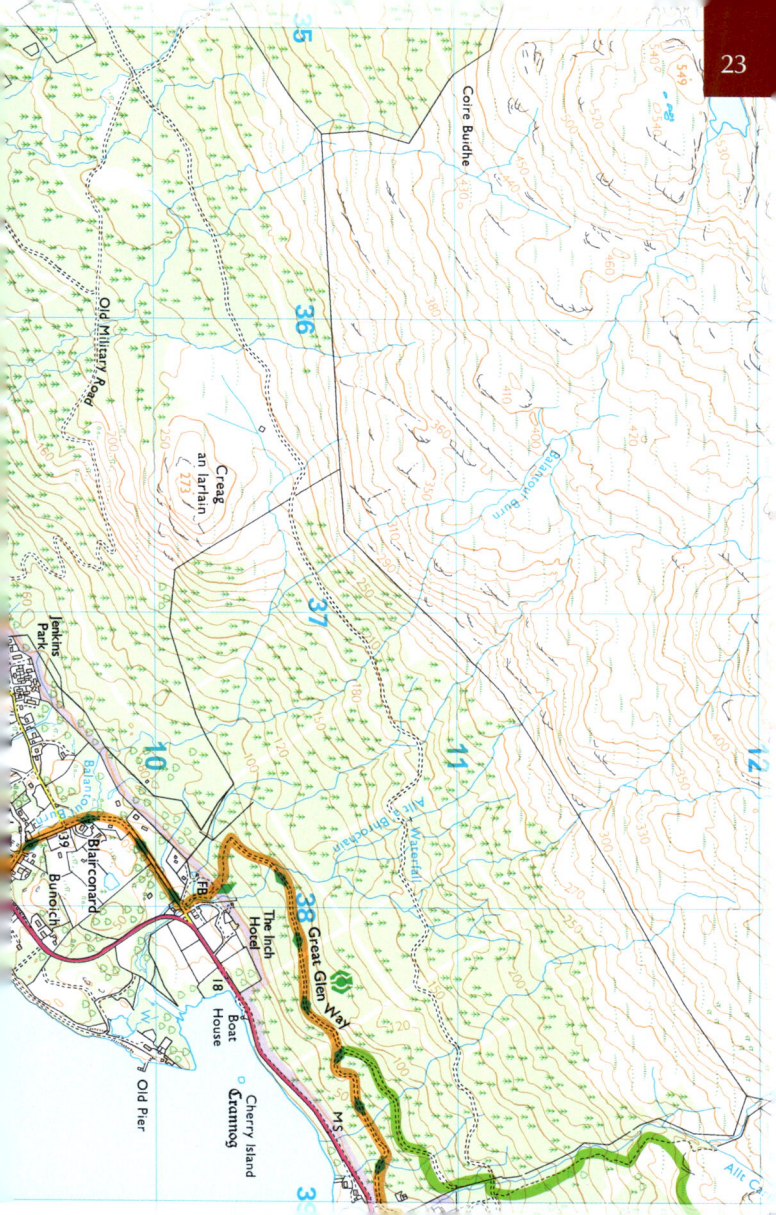

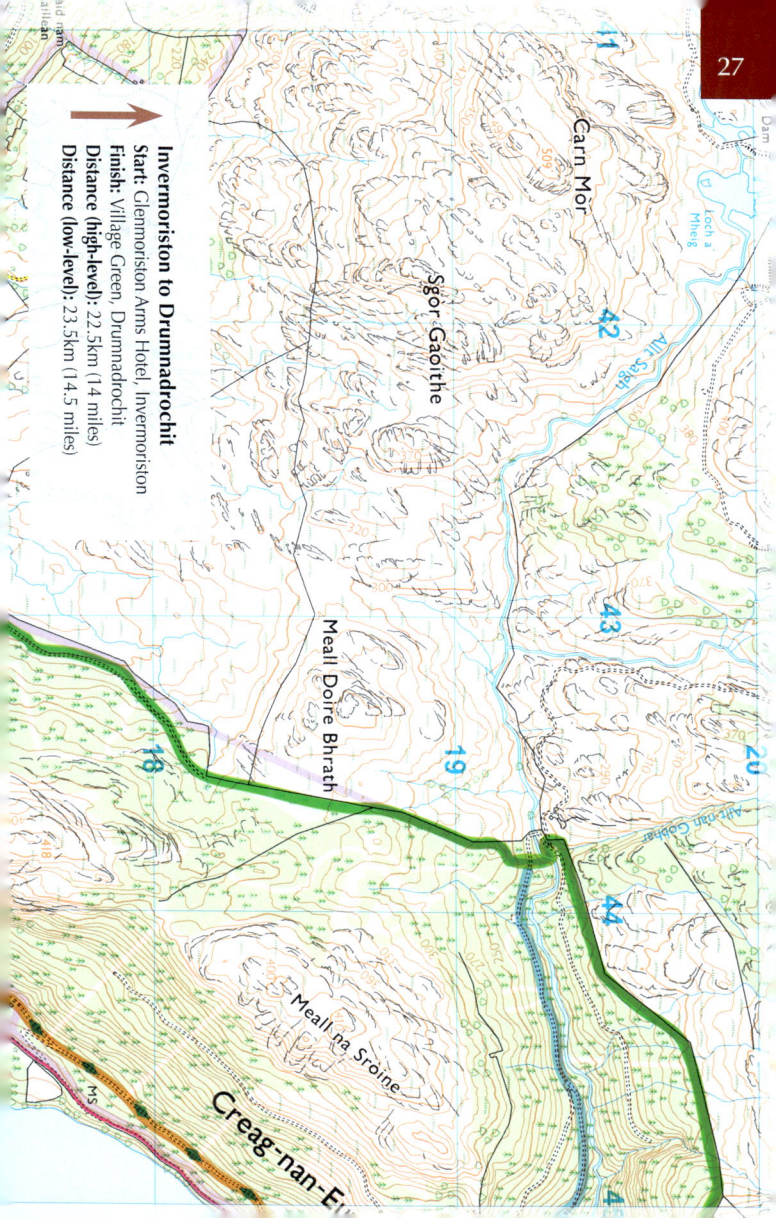

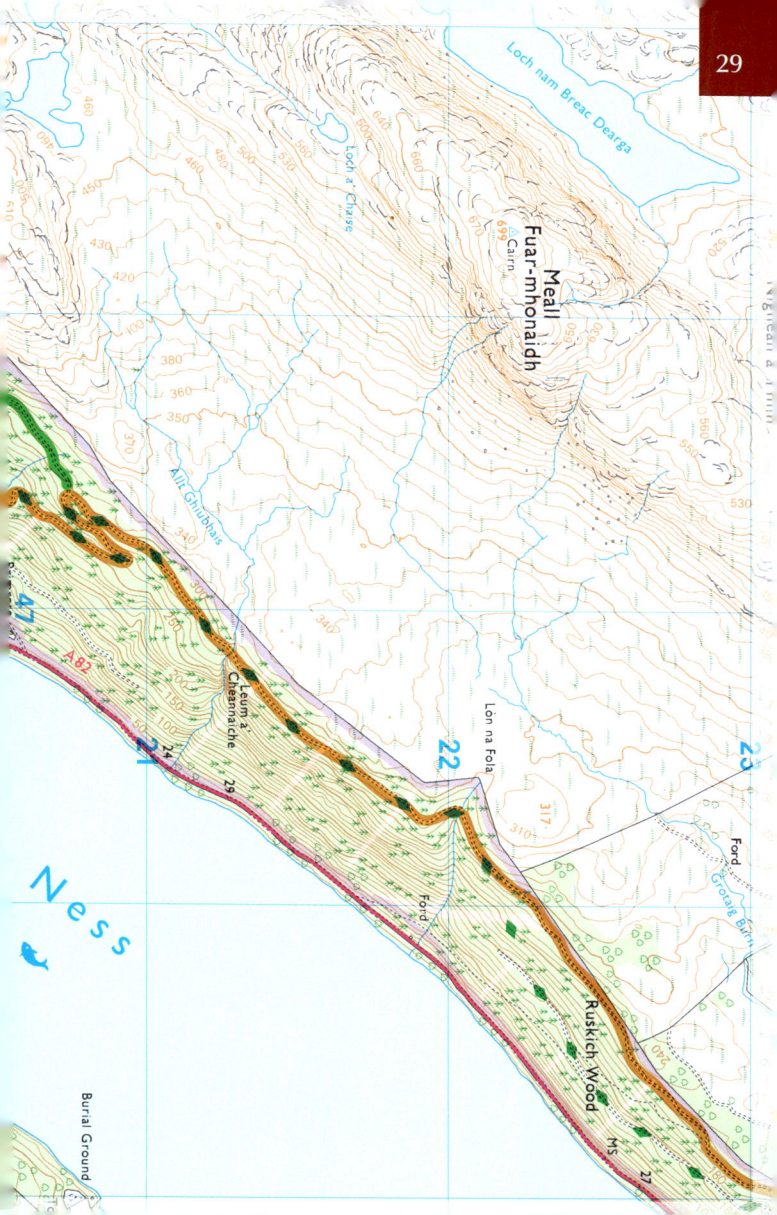

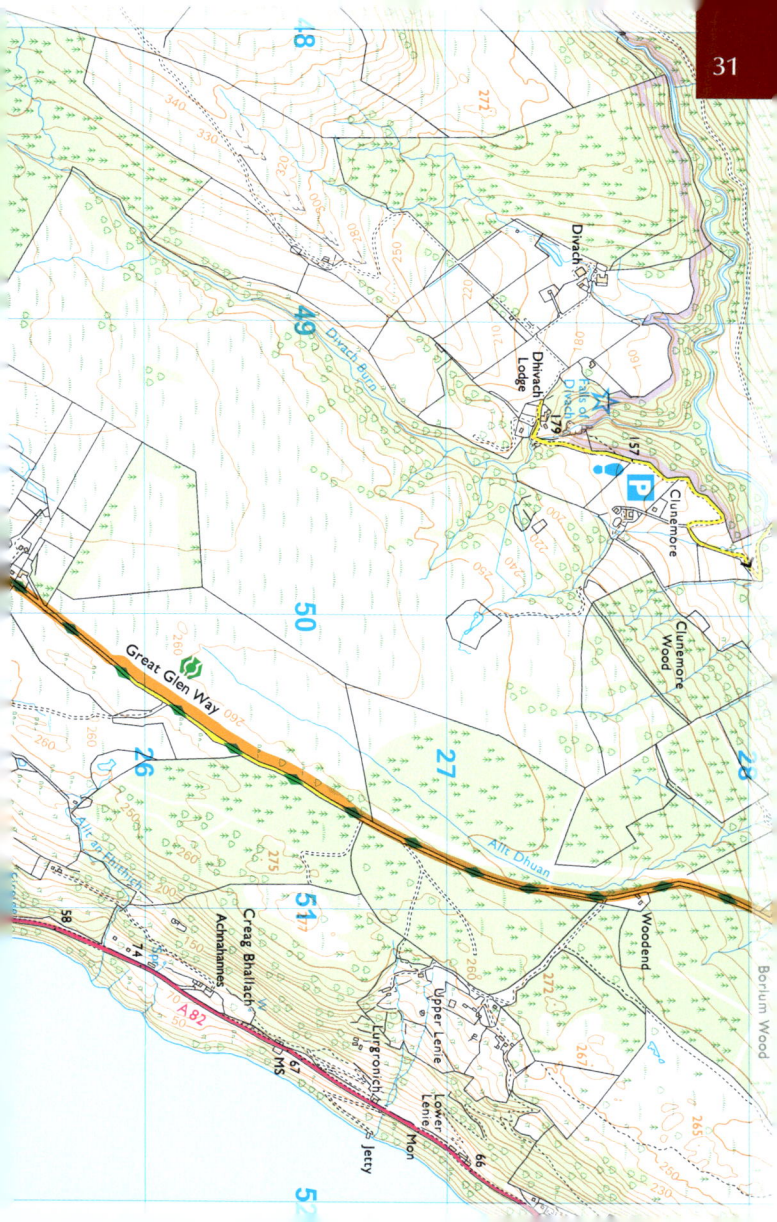

Drumnadrochit to Invermoriston
Start: Village Green, Drumnadrochit
Finish: Glenmoriston Arms Hotel, Invermoriston
Distance (high-level): 22.5km (14 miles)
Distance (low-level): 23.5km (14.5 miles)

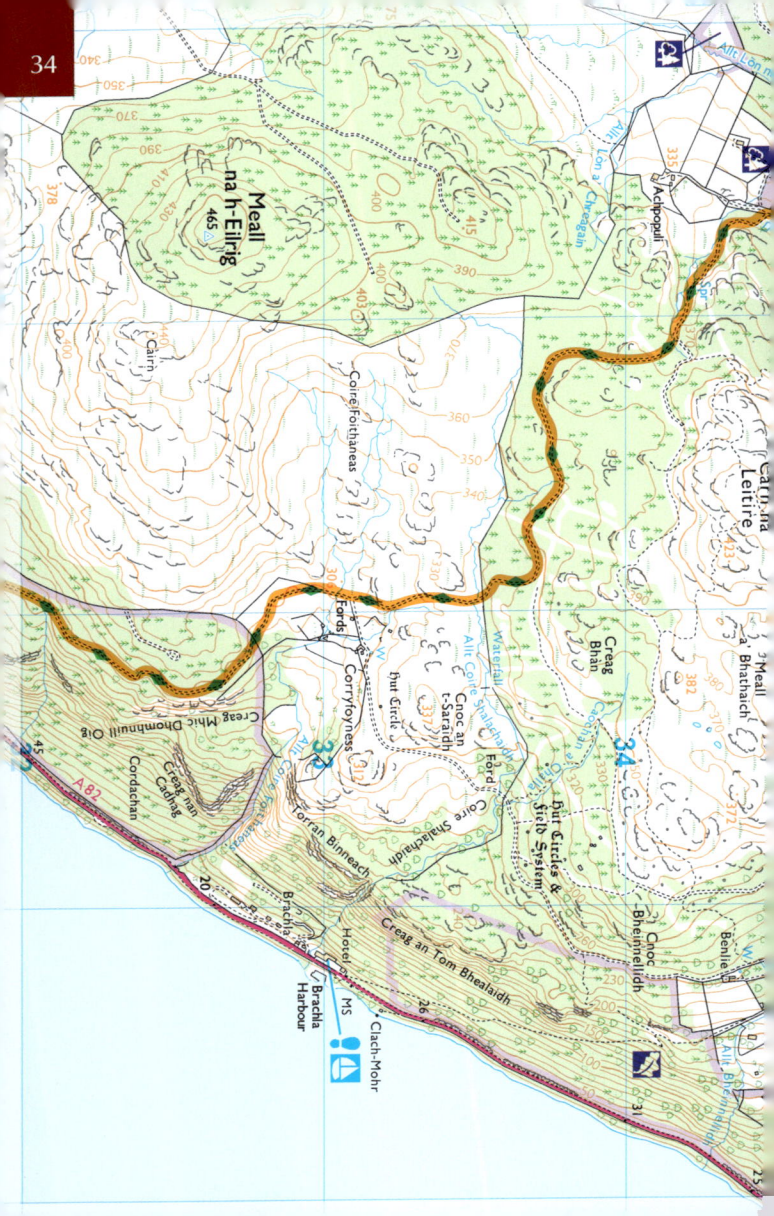

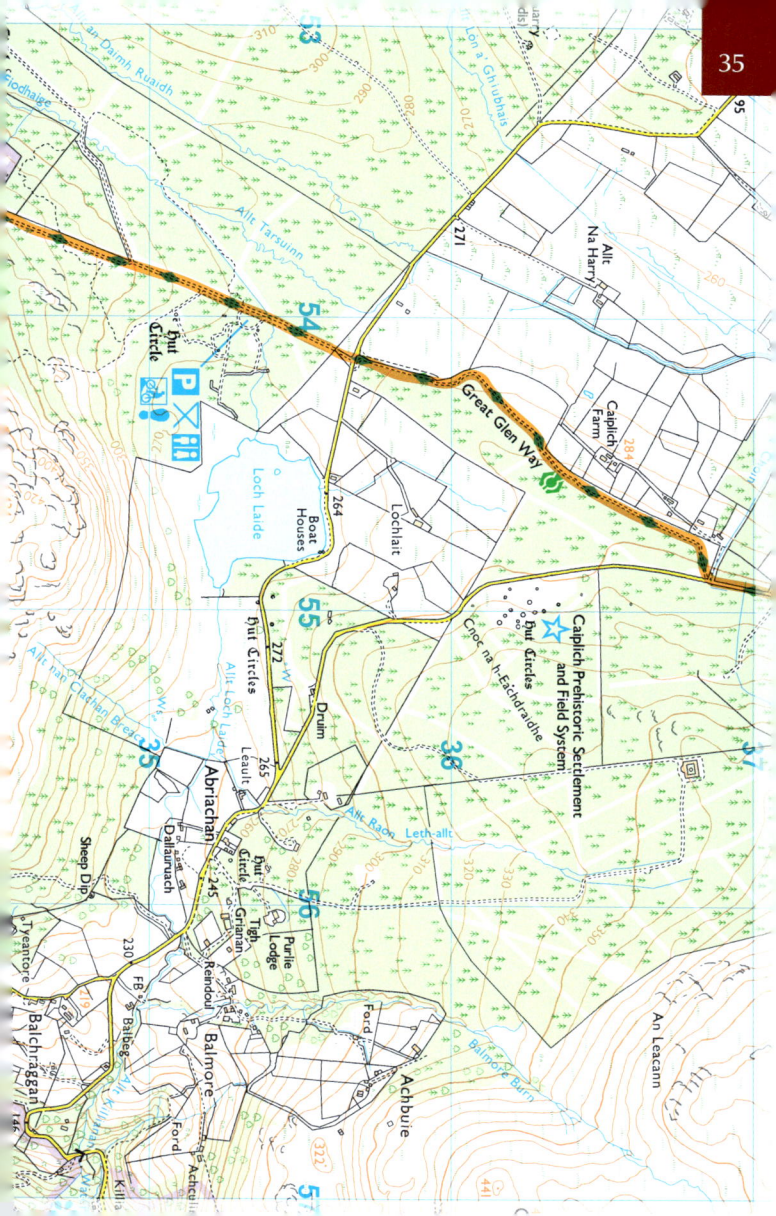

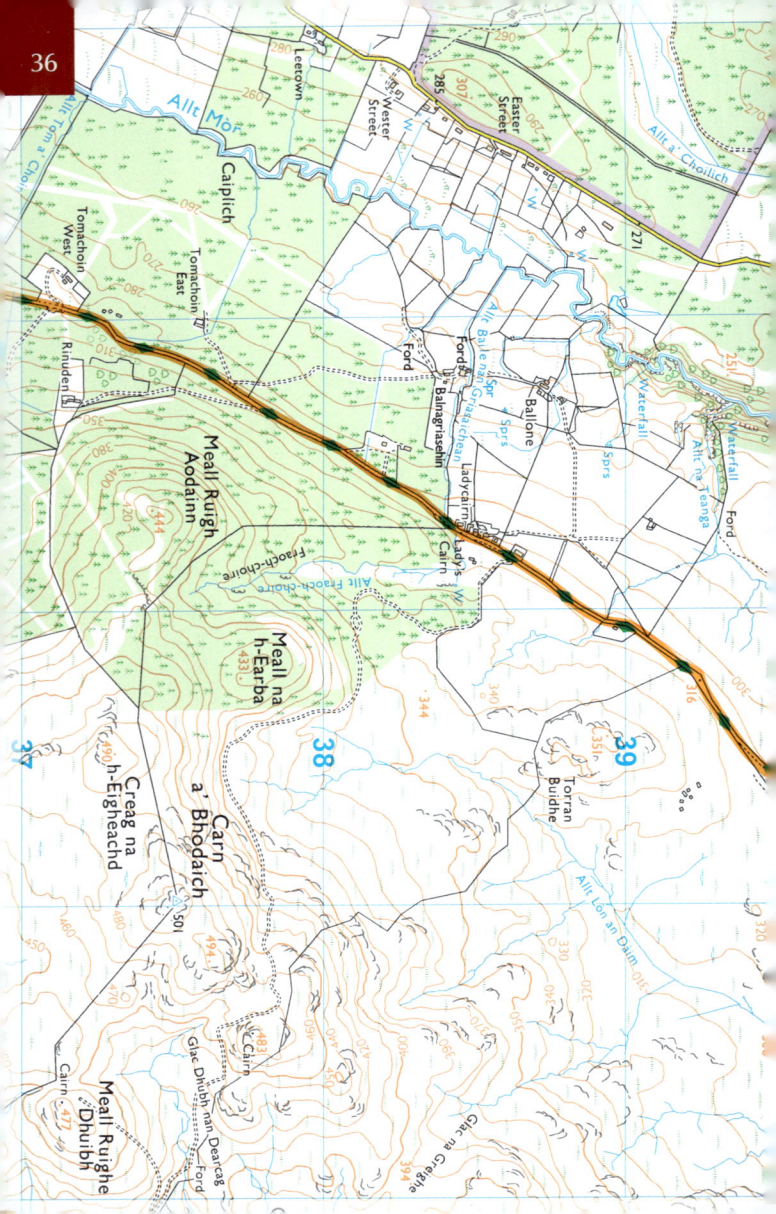

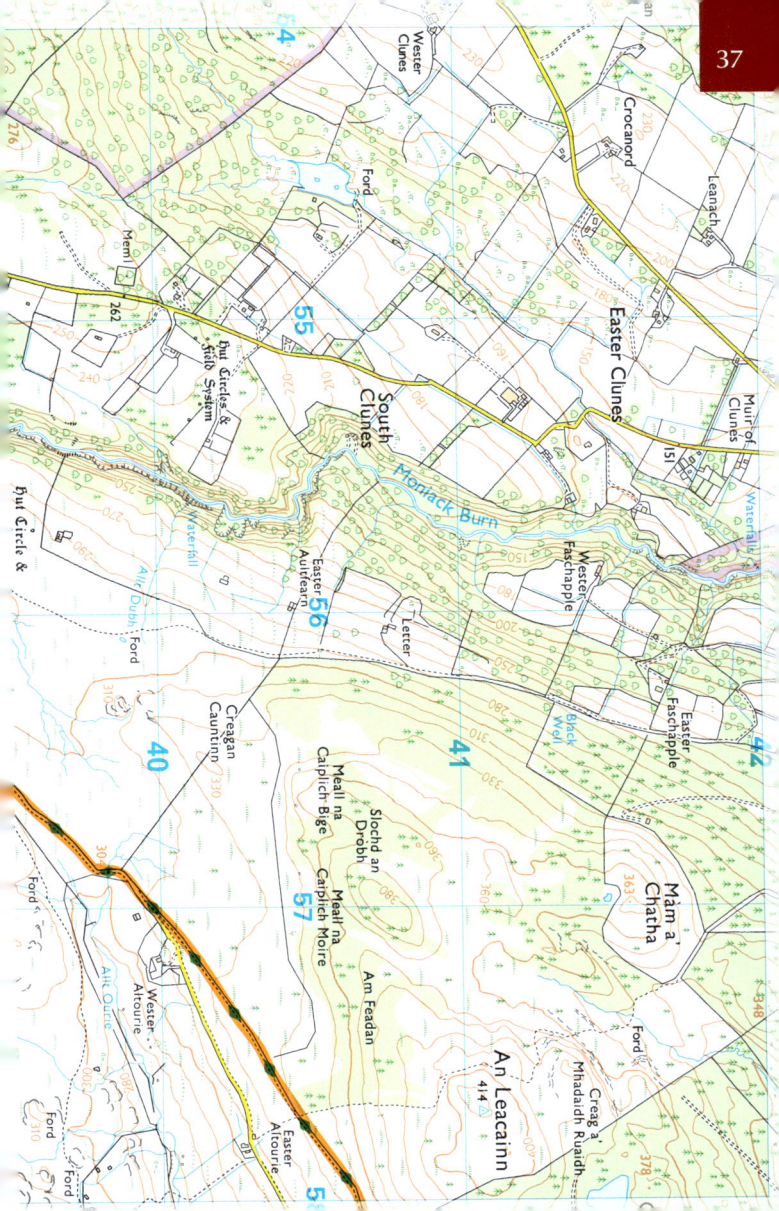

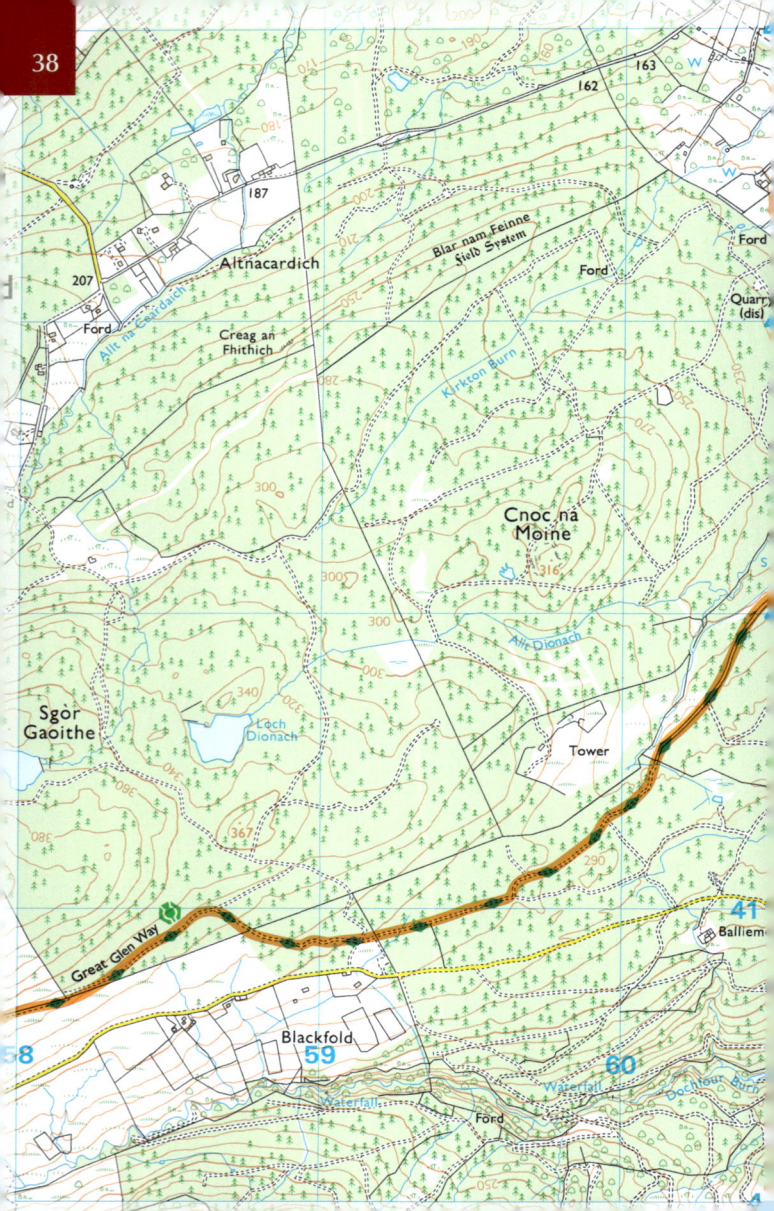

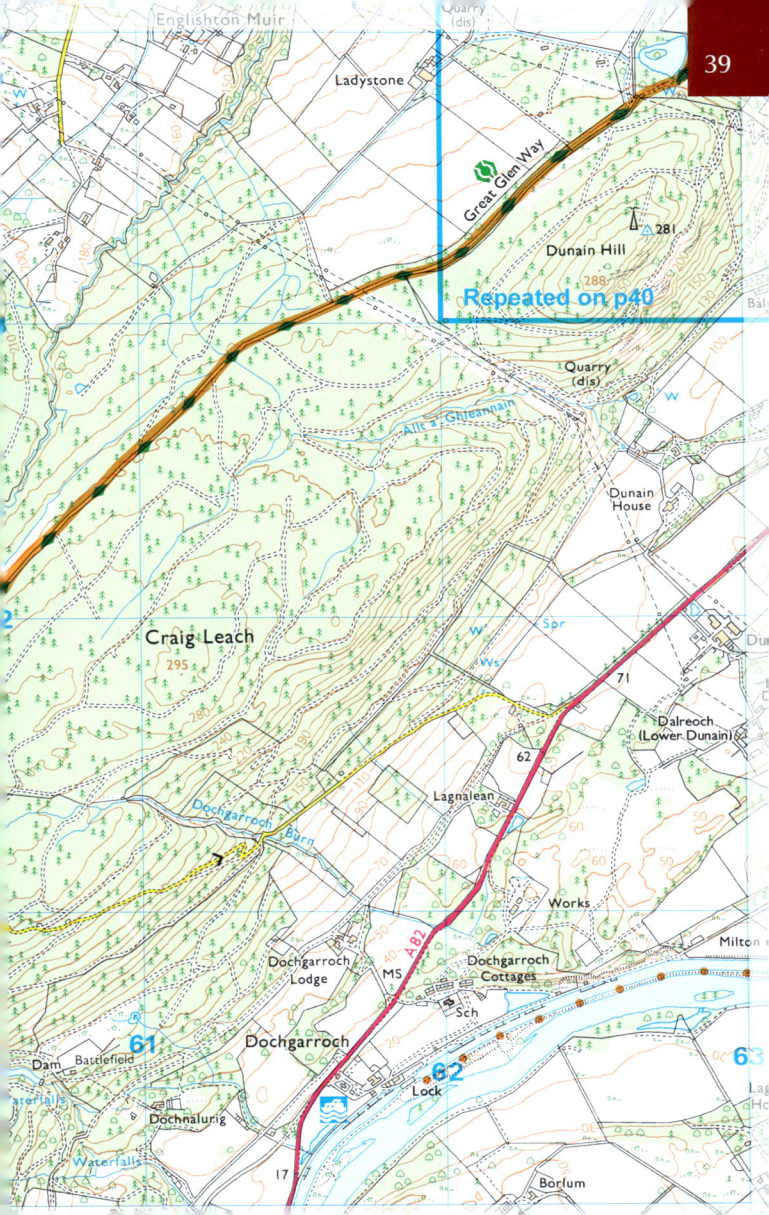

LEGEND OF SYMBOLS USED ON ORDNANCE SURVEY® 1:25,000 (EXPLORER) MAPPING

ROADS AND PATHS — Not necessarily rights of way

M1 or A6(M)	Motorway
	Service Area
	Junction Number (7)
A 35	Dual carriageway
A30	Main road
	Service Area
	Toll road junction (T1)
B 3074	Secondary road
	Narrow road with passing places
	Road under construction
	Road generally more than 4 m wide
	Road generally less than 4 m wide
	Other road, drive or track, fenced and unfenced
	Gradient: steeper than 20% (1 in 5); 14% (1 in 7) to 20% (1 in 5)
Ferry	Ferry; Ferry P – passenger only
	Path

RAILWAYS

- Multiple track / Single track — standard gauge
- Narrow gauge or Light rapid transit system (LRTS) and station
- Road over; road under; level crossing
- Cutting; tunnel; embankment
- Station, open to passengers; siding

PUBLIC RIGHTS OF WAY

- - - - - - - - Footpath
– – – – – Bridleway
+ + + + + Byway open to all traffic
– ‧ – ‧ – ‧ – Restricted byway

The representation on this map of any other road, track or path is no evidence of the existence of a right of way

ARCHAEOLOGICAL AND HISTORICAL INFORMATION

Symbol	Description	Symbol	Description	Symbol	Description
✣	Site of antiquity	VILLA	Roman	☆ ▦	Visible earthwork
⚔ 1066	Site of battle (with date)	Castle	Non-Roman		

Information provided by English Heritage for England and the Royal Commissions on the Ancient and Historical Monuments for Scotland and Wales

OTHER PUBLIC ACCESS

• • • Other routes with public access

The exact nature of the rights on these routes and the existence of any restrictions may be checked with the local highway authority. Alignments are based on the best information available

♦ ♦ ♦ Recreational route

♦ ♦ ♦ 🚶 National Trail   ⊕ Long Distance Route

- - - - - Permissive footpath ⎫
— — — — Permissive bridleway ⎭ Footpaths and bridleways along which landowners have permitted public use but which are not rights of way. The agreement may be withdrawn

• • • Traffic-free cycle route

[1] [1] National cycle network route number – traffic free; on road

ACCESS LAND

 Firing and test ranges in the area. Danger! Observe warning notices

 Access permitted within managed controls, for example, local byelaws. Visit www.access.mod.uk for information

Scotland

National Trust for Scotland, always open

National Trust for Scotland, limited access – observe local signs

Forestry Commission Land

Woodland Trust Land

In Scotland, everyone has access rights in law* over most land and inland water, provided access is exercised responsibly. **This includes walking, cycling, horse-riding and water access, for recreational and educational purposes, and for crossing land or water.** Access rights do not apply to motorised activities, hunting, shooting or fishing, nor if your dog is not under proper control. The **Scottish Outdoor Access Code** is the reference point for responsible behaviour, and can be obtained at www.outdooraccess-scotland.com or by phoning your local Scottish Natural Heritage office.

* Land Reform (Scotland) Act 2003

BOUNDARIES

— + — + National

— · — · County (England)

— — — — Unitary Authority (UA), Metropolitan District (Met Dist), London Borough (LB) or District (Scotland & Wales are solely Unitary Authorities)

· · · · · · · Civil Parish (CP) (England) or Community (C) (Wales)

━━ ━━ National Park boundary

VEGETATION

Limits of vegetation are defined by positioning of symbols

Coniferous trees

Non-coniferous trees

Coppice

Orchard

Scrub

Bracken, heath or rough grassland

Marsh, reeds or saltings

HEIGHTS AND NATURAL FEATURES

52 · Ground survey height
284 · Air survey height

Surface heights are to the nearest metre above mean sea level. Where two heights are shown, the first height is to the base of the triangulation pillar and the second (in brackets) to the highest natural point of the hill

Vertical face/cliff

Loose rock | Boulders | Outcrop | Scree

Contours are at 5 or 10 metre vertical intervals

- Water
- Mud
- Sand; sand and shingle

SELECTED TOURIST AND LEISURE INFORMATION

Building of historic interest	Nature reserve
Cadw	National Trust
Heritage centre	Other tourist feature
Camp site	Parking
Caravan site	Park and ride, all year
Camping and caravan site	Park and ride, seasonal
Castle / fort	Picnic site
Cathedral / Abbey	Preserved railway
Craft centre	Public Convenience
Country park	Public house/s
Cycle trail	Recreation / leisure / sports centre
Mountain bike trail	Roman site (Hadrian's Wall only)
Cycle hire	Slipway
English Heritage	Telephone, emergency
Fishing	Telephone, public
Forestry Commission Visitor centre	Telephone, roadside assistance
Garden / arboretum	Theme / pleasure park
Golf course or links	Viewpoint
Historic Scotland	Visitor centre
Information centre, all year	Walks / trails
Information centre, seasonal	World Heritage site / area
Horse riding	Water activites
Museum	Boat trips
National Park Visitor Centre (park logo) e.g. Yorkshire Dales	Boat hire

(For complete legend and symbols, see any OS Explorer map.)

Main photo: *A stack of five locks are passed as the Caledonian Canal enters Fort Augustus.*

The Great Glen Way

This map booklet accompanies the latest edition of Paddy Dillon's guidebook to walking the Great Glen Way. The route, including the Invergarry Link and high-level and low-level options between Fort Augustus and Drumnadrochit, is described in full from south to north and from north to south. The guidebook features annotated 1:100,000 mapping alongside detailed step-by-step route descriptions and full planning information.

Winter view across Loch Lochy from Bunarkaig (Stage 2, S–N; Stage 5, N–S)

OTHER CICERONE TRAIL GUIDES

 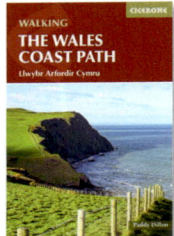 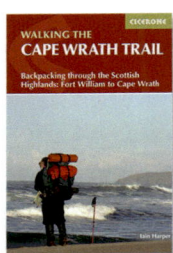

National Trails
The South West Coast Path
The South Downs Way
The North Downs Way
The Ridgeway National Trail
The Thames Path
The Cotswold Way
The Peddars Way and
  Norfolk Coast Path
The Cleveland Way and
  the Yorkshire Wolds Way
Cycling the Pennine Bridleway
The Pennine Way
Hadrian's Wall Path
The Pembrokeshire Coast Path
Offa's Dyke Path
Glyndŵr's Way

Scotland's Great Trails
The Southern Upland Way
The Speyside Way
The West Highland Way
The Great Glen Way

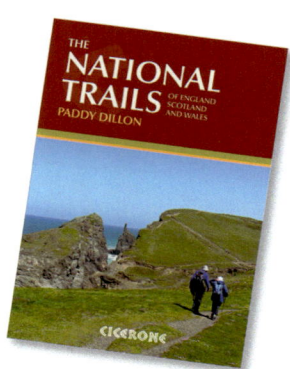

Visit our website for a full
list of Cicerone Trail Guides
www.cicerone.co.uk